ENJOY the RIDE

HOW TO EXPERIENCE THE TRUE JOY OF LIFE

THIS BOOK BELONGS · TO KAY McBRIDE

ENJOY the RIDE

HOW TO EXPERIENCE THE TRUE JOY OF LIFE

STEVE GILLILAND

INSIGHT PUBLISHING • SEVIERVILLE, TENNESSEE

Published by Insight Publishing Company
P.O. Box 4189
Sevierville, Tennessee 37864

Cover Design & Book Layout by Russ Hollingsworth
Edited by Marsha Shelton

Printed in the United States of America

ISBN 1-885640-55-2

DEDICATION

This book is affectionately dedicated to my sons,

Stephen and Josh.

May they always learn from their mistakes,

... and more importantly, from mine!

THE STATION

BY ROBERT HASTINGS

Tucked away in our subconscious is an idyllic vision. We see ourselves on a long trip that spans the continent. We are traveling by train. Out the windows, we drink in the passing scene of cars on nearby highways, of children waving at a crossing, of cattle grazing on a distant hillside, of smoke pouring from a power plant, of row upon row of corn and wheat, of flatlands and valleys, of mountains and rolling hillsides, of city skylines and village halls.

But uppermost in our minds is the final destination. On a certain day, at a certain hour, we will pull into the station. Bands will be playing and flags waving. Once we get there, so many wonderful dreams will come true and the pieces of our lives will fit together like a completed jigsaw puzzle. How restlessly we pace the aisles, damning the minutes for loitering—waiting, waiting, waiting for the station.

"When we reach the station, that will be it!" we cry. "When I'm 18." "When I buy a new 450SL Mercedes Benz." "When I put the last kid through college." "When I have paid off the mortgage!" "When I get a promotion."

"When I reach the age of retirement, I shall live happily ever after."

Sooner or later we must realize there is no station, no one place to arrive at once and for all. The true joy of life is the trip. The station is only a dream. It constantly outdistances us. "Relish the moment" is a good motto [especially when coupled with Psalm 118:24: "This is the day which the Lord hath made; we will rejoice and be glad in it"]. It isn't the burdens of today that drive men mad. It is the regrets over yesterday and the fear of tomorrow, twin thieves who rob us of today.

So stop pacing the aisles and counting the miles. Instead, climb more mountains, eat more ice cream, go barefoot more often, swim more rivers, watch more sunsets, laugh more, cry less. Life must be lived as we go along. The station will come soon enough.

CONTENTS

Acknowledgments.. xi

Welcome xiii

1 – CHECK YOUR PASSION
Don't Fear What You Want the Most... 1

2 – CURE YOUR DESTINATION DISEASE
Make "Now" the Most Interesting Time of All 11

3 – FOLLOW THE DIRECTIONS
At the Fork in the Road, Turn Right... 21

4 – REMEMBER THE RAINBOW
No One Can Ruin Your Day Without Your Permission 31

5 – DARE TO BE DIFFERENT
Comparison Prohibits You From Seeing Your Uniqueness 41

6 – REFOCUS YOUR ATTENTION
Decide What's Important and Never Take It For Granted...... 51

The ABC's For Your Trip.. 61

ACKNOWLEDGMENTS

I'd like to thank the many people who helped me while I was working on this book: from Performance Plus Professional Development, Inc., Marsha Broniszewski, Chris Procopio, Mike Murray, and my oldest son, Stephen.

I must say thank you to Marsha Shelton, my managing editor at Insight Publishing, for her patience and assistance as she worked through the manuscript.

Enjoy the Ride has also been deeply influenced by two men: my stepfather, Dave Wise, and my brother, Kim.

Finally, I want to thank my mother, Pat, who has had the greatest influence on my personal spiritual growth.

In memory of Margaret, my secretary,
1935 - 1994

WELCOME

We have already read that life is about strategies, habits, and rules. We have also been told, "Life isn't a destination, but rather a journey." Then we were told, "It's not how you start; it's more important how you finish." I personally have read some exceptional books by some exceptional authors and still keep coming back to one basic principle: Strategies, habits, rules, starts, and finishes are ALL determined by behaviors. These behaviors influence our choices, which ultimately decide our journey. Life's journey, which is our trip, requires us to make choices along the way. Regardless of who we are and where we are traveling, every day is filled with choices that ultimately determine whether we have inner peace and satisfaction at day's end.

For 39 years I strategically planned my life, exercised good and bad habits, and tried to live within the rules. In September, 1997, I woke up and realized that I wasn't consistently enjoying the journey and that my life had become a series of good days and bad days. As I began to look back on my life, I discovered that numerous choices I had made had altered my journey, and the bad days had begun to outweigh the good days. I realized that my choices were a direct result of my behavior and that I needed a remedy, or treatment, if you will. My behavior was a result of numerous influences that were set in motion early in life and affirmed along the way. In addition, I realized that inner peace involves making good decisions and setting the right priorities. It comes from building lasting, genuine, and healthy relationships. You're only as rich as your relationships. It doesn't stem from loving things and using people, but from loving people and using things. It comes from making genuine, permanent commitments in marriage and forming lasting, unconditional relationships with your kids, your loved ones, and your friends.

This book is my gift to everyone who is searching for an inner peace. I firmly believe that the true joy of life is the trip and that in order to enjoy the ride we have to change our behavior through choices we make every day. For some, that will be easy, and after reading the book you will begin to see the results. For others, it will take a daily reminder or, in essence, someone to ride with you and hold you accountable – a friend, family member, or co-worker with whom you are willing to share and be vulnerable. Many people who read this book will learn something; unfortunately, only a few will use it. My prayer is that you continue your life's journey learning from the lessons you are given every day, realizing the only consequence for resisting lessons is that they will keep repeating themselves until you learn them.

1

CHECK YOUR PASSION

Don't Fear What You Want the Most

Your life's work can be found where God's plan
intersects with your passion.

I have just returned from my annual performance review and my secretary, Margaret, inquires regarding the outcome. With no excitement in my voice, I tell her that once again I have exceeded expectations and achieved yet another bonus and the top-grade merit raise. Sensing my lack of enthusiasm, she enters my office and asks, "If every job in the world paid the same, would you still be our sales manager? What I am asking is, would you still be our sales manager, or would you be happier, more energized, or love doing something different if all jobs paid the same?"

I grinned and said, "At the risk of losing my job and sounding ungrateful, no."

"What would you do?"

"I would be in front of an audience motivating them to maximize their potential, inspiring them to focus on their talents, and teaching them new skills and competencies. I would be traveling the world sharing my heart."

Without hesitation she then said, "So what's stopping you?"

My response was simple: "Do a 401K program, direct deposit, quarterly bonus plan, great salary, and great position mean anything to you?"

"Not really! If I wake up every day and don't have any passion towards what I am doing, forget why I'm doing it, and hate who I'm doing it with, then it's time to check my passion."

Love what you do; love why you do it;
love whom you do it with.

It would be through Margaret's keen discernment and loving encouragement that I would resign my position and begin to pursue my passion. So let me ask you that same question and rephrase it a little: If every job in the world paid the same, or shall we say, $2 an hour, where would you work? Think about it. No matter what the job, what would you do if every job paid the same? Would you still be doing what you are currently doing? Have you ever thought about why you selected your current career or job? Remember when you were in high school and everyone asked, "Have you thought about what you are going to do after graduation?" I meet people every day who tell me they would be doing something different if everything paid the same. I understand their answer; however, I find myself thinking about my own life and the reasons I was working where I was, when I was. Ask yourself this question: Is my current life direction based on my expectations or someone else's? We all have a passion or desire for something in life, and too many times instead of being encouraged to pursue it, or even helped, we are not. Our passion is sometimes put aside to pursue the world's definition of success. Where we live, what we drive, and how many material possessions we have are the cornerstones of our decision-making process.

Abundance is the result of appreciation not accumulation.

And how many of us have worked at good jobs not even realizing why we do what we do every day? After high school our family and friends are asking, "Have you found a good job yet?" Why is it we are searching for a good job instead of looking for our life's work that fits our passion? Could it be that if we pursued what we really loved and desired, our parents would have a tough time explaining or interacting with friends and family about our careers? We sit around talking to complete strangers about our children and family members, bragging about where they are and what they are doing as long as it falls into the world's definition of success.

It's tragic to think that people will work all of their lives doing something they moderately enjoy for the sake of someone else's approval. Some people wake up every day with no desire to go to work and feel empty most days because they realize that they never pursued their passion. We have a house, two cars, and all that the world has to offer materially, yet miss the most important element of life – inner peace. In addition, we follow other people's expectations and mistake that for our passion. We get married because we think it is the right thing to do. We then have children after marriage because we think it is the right thing to do. We miss their Little League games to make ends meet and rationalize it's the right thing to do. We drop them off at child care so we can make enough money to give them what we never had. When we finally give it to them, we realize why we never had it; our parents knew it wasn't what we needed. We replace a bedtime story with 30 more minutes on the computer. We replace breakfast with a Pop-Tart. We replace the school bus with a car. We replace home-work with home shopping. We replace talking to our children with a chat room. We replace Andy Griffith with COPS. We re-place Father Knows Best with Big Brother. We give them a bike instead of a book and a car instead of a curfew. We don't have the courage to tell them no, but we expect them to "just say no." We pay for a baby-sitter to go out because we say we deserve it. We stop calling our parents and visiting as often. When the next technological wave of inventions arrives, we buy all of them. We have no satisfaction until we have them, or so we think. We complain of debt and how tight money is, yet we own two cars and both of them are financed. We purchase new shoes but never discard the old pair and never wear them again. We never pack our lunch or come home and just sit on the porch. We skip breakfast, lunch, and eat fast food for din-ner. Our lives are in the fast lane with no exit ramp in sight. We do it because everyone else does and live beyond our means to support someone else's meaning.

We purchase things we don't need,
with money we don't have,
to impress people we don't even like.

So why do we do it? Why do we pursue so many things that leave us so empty instead of chasing after our passion? What we want the most we fear, because it may not be what someone else sees us doing. Our relationships, our careers, and our toys are sometimes a reflection of the dysfunctional approach we take to life based on everything but our own desires. We succumb to the pressure of so many opinions other than our own. I recently sat on a flight from San Antonio to Dallas beside a woman who answered my $2 question with a smile on her face and passionate tears in her eyes. When she was 15 and a student nurse, she befriended a woman who would eventually die with cancer. It was at that point she knew her passion was to work with cancer patients for the rest of her life. Against her parents desire, she would go on to spend the next 40 years doing just that, being a nurse waking up every day, loving what she did, loving why she did it, and loving whom she did it with. She never desired to get married or even have children. Her mother and father were doctors and, as she explained, "never totally accepted me after I refused to go to medical school."

Our choices should be based on our talents and passion. It's worth noting that our passion can be threatened by the lack of leadership that exists in so many companies. For example, a person who has a desire to take care of people and loves being around people follows her passion and becomes a nurse. However, she soon realizes that 75% of her time is spent doing paperwork and only 25% of her time is spent using her talent – taking care of people. And what about those of you who are reading this and saying, "It's not that easy. I have a mortgage, children, and responsibilities; I just can't walk away from my current position and start over." No one said you could; however, it is very motivating to know that you can begin to develop a long-term plan to gradually put you where you want to be.

You will never leave where you are until you decide where you would rather be.

At times we make a bad choice, and that choice brings on a feeling of obligation. This obligation makes us fearful, which in turn leads us to more bad choices. Again, our fears can be traced back to expectations, usually someone else's. After speaking in Charleston, South Carolina, on the subject of "Managing Multiple Priorities: How to Get Organized and Achieve Balance in Your Life," a woman approached me and told me a story that affirmed how we sometimes live to appease others and put our desires second. During a break, she shared with me that on her wedding night her husband beat her up. When I asked her what she did, her response was, "When you come from a small town, you don't get back from your honeymoon and file for divorce." Isn't it tragic to know what to do and yet feel powerless to pursue it? Her fears were based on everyone else's expectations, and as a result she stayed married for six years in an abusive relationship – six years of her trip without ever Enjoying the Ride!

The trip is more enjoyable if you know where you're going.

Just recently our youngest son, Josh, returned home to Pennsylvania from his freshman year at college in Florida. He was attending on a baseball scholarship and majoring in communication. He has always been a talented athlete. In high school he lettered in football, basketball, and baseball in his sophomore, junior, and senior years. In the midst of his fall semester at college, I visited him to see how he was adjusting to being so far from home. He assured me he wasn't homesick. In addition, he told me he was doing all right in his classes; however, just like in high school, he wasn't enjoying any of them. When I asked why, he said, "I went to college, but it wasn't what I really wanted to do, and yet everyone told me I would be crazy to pass up on the opportunity to play baseball at college in Florida. I guess what I'm saying, Dad, is that I'm only doing this because I figured it was what you would want me to do." POW! How is that for a lesson on learning what I try to teach others? Amazed and puzzled, I then asked the $2 question, to which he replied with tears in his eyes, "All my life I have dreamed about either working on one or driving one – Dad, I want to be a part of racing."

Astonished and a little bit sick to my stomach, I told him I needed time to think about his announcement. As I normally did, I sought my mother's advice. Her words surprised me: "If Josh wakes up every day and loves what he does, is a good citizen, a good neighbor, a loving father, and only makes $15,000 a year, then what is to say he is not successful?" POW! Defining success is a difficult task. Most people equate it with wealth, power, and happiness. But true success is not a thing you acquire or achieve. Rather, it is a journey you take your whole life long. Incredible as it may seem, Josh checked his passion at age 20 and isn't looking back.

So where do you fit into this picture? When you reflect on where you are presently at, where you have been, and where you are headed, are you really enjoying the ride? The beginning of the trip for some doesn't come at birth; it only begins when your passion is found and followed. What you make of your life is up to you. You have all the tools and resources you need. What you do with them is up to you. Your passion helps you realize the authorship of your life. So many people excuse the idea that they have the power to script their own lives. They blame circumstances or their inability to attain the proper resources. Fortunately, our success is not determined by external resources but rather by our willingness to create a life according to our highest passion and belief in ourselves.

There are no limits in life.

Passion moves mountains, and when combined with faith, courage, and power, it takes people to places they have dared to dream about. Faith becomes the single source for light when everything around you appears so dark. It simply believes without tangible proof. One thing I have personally realized is that to restore my faith during the toughest times I have surrounded myself with people who are familiar with my authenticity and keep me rooted in my beliefs. My inner circle of friends and my mother keep me on track. Passion without faith can sabotage your dreams. But what keeps you moving when you follow your passion and your faith propels you in the right direction? Courage is the energy source that ignites your plans and moves you forward during your trip. Courage is learned in the moment that you take a leap of faith and follow your passion. I will never forget what an officer in the United States Marine Corps said to me after I finished speaking at Parris Island. He said, "The reason why some recruits never become United States Marines is that they never get on or off the bus." He then proceeded to show me the yellow boot prints that are painted in the pavement where the new recruits stand when they depart the bus that brings them to Parris Island for the very first time. He stated, "What separates every recruit is the courage it takes to board the bus after they have decided to join the Marines, or to get off the bus when they finally arrive."

What fears stand in your way? You have checked your passion, realize what it is, yet remain paralyzed in relationships, careers, and situations that are within your control. There are many times you have difficulty seeing the power that lies within you. You need to call on your own inner strength in order to pursue your passion. The only things that stops you are rejection and disappointment, which all too often accompany you on your journey. Earlier in this chapter I told the story of the young woman who returned home after her wedding and felt powerless. Power means demonstrating your ability to manifest reality. Is it easy? If it were, I wouldn't have waited until I was 39 to pursue my passions. I wouldn't have waited 44 years to write this book. I personally enjoyed many parts of my journey before age 44; however, I truly never consistently enjoyed the ride until I checked my passion and began fitting all the pieces together. So I ask you again: Why do we pursue so many things that leave us so empty instead of chasing after our passion? I encourage you to trust yourself and explore all the options. Thanks to a wonderful secretary, Margaret Shannon, I checked my passion, trusted my choices, and realized that if I am diligent, everything is possible.

2

CURE YOUR DESTINATION DISEASE

Make "Now" the Most Interesting Time of All

---

*Live more for today, less for tomorrow,
and never about yesterday.*

It was time for our family's annual vacation to Myrtle Beach, a journey of more than thirteen hours from the outskirts of Pittsburgh, Pennsylvania. Our plan was to leave at 2 a.m. on Saturday so we could drive straight through and check into our condominium by 3 p.m. After all, I had paid a hefty deposit for the week and was told we could check in anytime after 3 p.m., so I wasn't going to waste a minute. When we would finally get to Myrtle Beach, we would all, at the request of me, unpack and get settled in prior to going to the beach. Actually, we would never make it to the beach our first day because we would run out of time before we had to go to dinner. The week would entail me getting up, cooking breakfast, and informing everyone of lunch plans, dinner plans, and what we might do that evening. Sounds like fun, right? Looking back I realize that I spent so much time thinking about what was next

I never enjoyed what was now. My sons recently confessed that our vacations were always about what we were going to do next instead of "chilling out and enjoying now."

Earlier in the book I placed a copy of Robert Hastings' "The Station." In this wonderful piece, Hastings reveals the greatest fact of life: there is no destination – "it constantly outdistances us." I have had the privilege of being around some very success- ful people who all agree on one thing. At the height of their success, they never truly enjoyed it because they were always thinking about what was next. Recently, on a flight from Jack- sonville, Florida, to San Francisco, California, I had the oppor- tunity to discuss this very thing with an elderly gentleman who had just celebrated his ninety-seventh birthday. We talked about life in the Roaring Twenties and the depression of the thirties. But what hit me the hardest was his response to this question: If you could live your life over again and change one thing, what would you change? He said, "Young man, if I could change one thing, I would have lived more for the day and less for tomorrow. I buried my wife thirty-one years ago and have outlived all three of my children. A few years before I retired, I remember thinking how I never enjoyed the ride to work be- cause I was always thinking about what I had to do when I got to work. If I could do it again, this time I would drive a differ- ent way to work every day just to enjoy the commute more. During my first break I was always thinking about what I had to do when I got back from my break. At lunch time I ate some great food, enjoyed some great fellowship with my co-workers, but uppermost in my mind were the tasks that lay ahead after my lunch was finished. On the way home from work I was al- ways thinking about what I had to do when I got home. At din- ner I found myself thinking about what needed doing when I finished eating. Many times when I laid my head on my pillow I would be thinking about the next morning. Young man, what

I'm trying to say is that I lived my life fifteen minutes ahead every day."

If tomorrow never comes, would you be satisfied with the way today ended?

As he continued talking, all I could think about was how many days I have been thirty minutes ahead, not enjoying the moment. I, too, remember saying things like, I'll be so glad when they're out of Little League (referring to my two sons), and if I can just get them through high school.... So many times I planned for the future and, unfortunately, lived in it too. And how many times did I hurry to get someplace else so that I didn't enjoy the moment at hand. Even a simple trip through a drive-through would reveal my inability to focus on an enjoyable moment and turn it into a function of existence that needed to be accomplished only for survival. Even when one son desired McDonald's while the other lobbied for Wendy's, I would be insistent on them picking one or the other. I think back to those days and now long for them to be in the car wanting to stop at both, but at ages 23 and 21 those days are nothing more than a memory.

We all seemingly suffer from this illusionary disease that has our minds focused on the future while we exist in the present. I personally know people who despise Mondays and really don't begin to enjoy the week until they reach the "over-the-hump" day of Wednesday. Sad, but true; anyone who doesn't enjoy Mondays misses one-seventh of their life. We wake up in the morning complaining about what lies ahead instead of enjoying each breath we take now. From the shower to shaving our thoughts begin to unravel our day and even our tomorrow, which may never come. We rush through breakfast, wake the kids, and dart off to another day, missing so much of a morning that was meant to be relished with moments that create memories. No disrespect to any brand of coffee, but the best part of waking up is waking up. When is the last time you spent two or more hours of your morning at home awake prior to departing for work? When is the last time you were assembled around the breakfast table with your entire family? When is the last time you spent fifteen minutes on the front porch drinking a cup of coffee or tea prior to your departure to work? If you're like many, you can't remember when, and if you do remember, it probably wasn't all too familiar because of the infrequency. Remember the 97-year-old gentleman? He said he would have spent more time in the mornings enjoying his family, his porch, and some quiet time. He also said he would have never again skipped lunch or worked through it thinking about what lay ahead.

Start from where you are now.

It is this destination disease that affects our outlook, attitude, and emotional well-being. Fridays rob us of our Mondays, just as dessert spoils our dinner. I am a firm believer that we must plan our future; however, the challenge is not to live in it. In 2001 I was waiting for a flight to depart Kansas City with my final destination being Indianapolis. As I began to pull out my computer, the Southwest Airlines gate agent began making an announcement. "This announcement is for anyone traveling on the flight to Indianapolis. Due to a maintenance problem, we are looking at a delay of around two hours. Mechanics are on board right now assessing the problem. When I have more information available, I will let you know." Within seconds of the announcement ending, people were livid and began acting out their frustration – papers slamming, people cussing, and cell phones dialing; the entire gate area was consumed with people who were visibly angry. As I sat and observed them, I remembered the days when I, too, would have become angered and agitated.

For every sixty seconds you're angry you lose one minute of happiness.

What was the key to my calmness? No more Destination Disease. I, too, wanted to get to Indianapolis; however, I quickly realized that the next two hours of my life was about choices. I could either be positive or negative, dwell on something I couldn't control, or keep myself busy and enjoy the extra time in Kansas City. As I sat observing several people, I noticed a little girl who was probably between three and four years old, sitting on the floor in front of her mother, who was on her cell phone. To the right of the child's mother was an elderly woman reading the newspaper, and at her feet was a small vinyl dog carrier with a little schnauzer in it. Without notice, the mother paused from her phone conversation, looked down at her daughter, and shouted, "I expect you to eat all of those mashed potatoes while we're stuck in this stupid airport." The elderly woman reading the paper looked down at the little girl with an affirming look, as if to say, "And you better do what your mother says." With that, the little girl proceeded to open a container of KFC mashed potatoes with a disappointed look on her face. After opening the potatoes, I simultaneously noticed the same thing she did – the little schnauzer. Now her look of disappointment turned to a sheepish grin as she proceeded to feed the dog her mashed potatoes. I, too, grinned and prayed that neither her mother nor the elderly woman would catch her in the act. After she finished, she proudly showed the mother the empty container and her mother replied, "If you ate like that all the time, we wouldn't have the problems we do at dinner time." I continued to enjoy the carefree behavior and innocence of the little girl, realizing that she had not yet reached an age where destinations had taken over her life.

> *By always chasing after another "there" you are never really appreciating what you already have right here.*

Many people believe that once you arrive at wherever your "there" is, you will finally become happy, generous, loving, and content. What happens is that you constantly long for something else and never allow yourself the joy of the present. You are constantly being torn between setting your goals, dreaming, and your enjoyment of your life right now. Your challenge is to focus on the present and on what you have right now, while simultaneously holding the intention of your future goals.

One of the ways in which you can begin to enjoy what is instead of what might be is to cultivate a heart of appreciation. It is too easy to focus on what we hope to obtain and overlook the gifts we already have. Imagine what your life would be like if you lost all that you had. I am always reminded of the great seventeenth-century violinist, Niccolo Paganini, and the lesson he left behind while performing a concert one evening. He was playing his violin when suddenly a string broke. Much to the surprise of everyone he continued to play his violin with only three strings. In amazement the audience continued to marvel at his ability to play on the three remaining strings. However, due to the pressure he was placing on the remaining three strings another string snapped. Without stopping, he shut his eyes and continued ever so slowly to pull his bow across the two strings, never playing a sour note. At the end of his concert he made one final emphatic push of his bow upward across the two remaining strings and another one snapped. The crowd went crazy. They stood, cheered, and seemingly realized that they had just witnessed the most amazing display of musical magic ever performed. Paganini, however, wasn't done. With the crowd standing in amazement, he stood silently and motioned for them to be seated. He then stood on his chair and raised his arms, with his bow in one hand and his violin in the other, and proclaimed, "I have never yet performed a concert without giving an encore, and tonight will be no different. Ladies and gentlemen, Paganini...and one string!" He played his one-stringed violin for another five minutes. At the end he simply bowed and left the stage. So let me ask, when would you have stopped playing? Paganini taught us all something that evening.

It's not the broken strings that stop you; it's your inability to see what you have left to play.

Your focus so many times is on what you want or what you've lost without even realizing what is most important – what you have. Many people are afraid of not having enough of whatever it is they need or want, so they are always striving towards a destination where they believe they will have enough. They fool themselves into believing that some day they will have all the money they need, all the possessions they desire, all the love they crave, and all the success they strive for. Late in life they come to the realization that it was never enough and there is no destination. So take a minute to think about everything you have and where you are. You have a loving marriage, health, good friends, and so many other free things that cost you nothing but are truly priceless.

Something else that makes the present so powerful is the inner peace it offers. When you live in the moment, you aren't reliving the past or fearing the future. Your past is made of regret and resentment, while your future is made up of uncertainty. Your present offers no expectations, only the realities of the moment. I remember what a friend of mine, who is a professional counselor, one time said: "Make your life a series of moments that when multiplied transform into a series of memories." My translation – you'll never remember what you never experienced. So many people are so focused on what's next they miss so much of what's now. I fly virtually every week. If you were to ask ten passengers sitting on an airplane headed to Charlotte, North Carolina, what they were doing, nine of them would most likely respond, "I'm on my way to Charlotte." The tenth one who responds, "I'm reading a great book," is the one who has learned the lesson of present peace.

I'm not suggesting that you completely detach yourself from the past and stay blind to the future. I am a firm believer in setting goals, planning, and pursuing your passions. I am suggesting that in order to enjoy the ride you must pursue your passion and plan for it, but don't live beyond the moment that gives you the true joy. Paul McCartney of the Beatles was quoted as saying, "We never really enjoyed our success because we were always focused on what was next." I, too, have been guilty of that same thing. Remember as a child asking, "Are we there yet?" Sometimes you started asking while you were still in the driveway. Children certainly have a harder time knowing where they are on a trip than adults do . . . or do they? On a recent flight from Charlotte to Los Angeles, I was sitting in my seat trying to finish up a project I had been working on, when the flight attendant announced that we were starting to make our initial descent into LAX airport. I could hear everyone around me packing up belongings, putting away magazines, and getting ready to deplane. But I kept working. I knew I had several minutes before I needed to put my files back in my briefcase and get ready to leave the plane. You see, even as adults we often ride like children, impatiently missing the present to arrive in the future. "So stop pacing the aisles and counting the miles. Instead, climb more mountains, eat more ice cream [chocolate chip cookie dough], go barefoot more often, swim more rivers, watch more sunsets, laugh more, and cry less. Life must be lived as we go along. The destination will always outdistance you."

3

FOLLOW THE DIRECTIONS

At the Fork in the Road, Turn Right

For every action or event, there is an accompanying lesson that must be learned.

When you come to the fork in the road, always turn right. How do you know you should turn right? Simple; whenever you go right, you can't go wrong. Haven't you heard the saying "I just wish life came with a set of instructions"? Ironically, it does; unfortunately, we choose not to follow them. By nature we would rather produce excuses instead of providing results. We refuse to take ownership of our roles in certain situations, yet the problems, circumstances, and conditions we face are a result of not following the directions. As simple as it sounds, it is also very, very powerful. Too many times when we are faced with a decision, a "fork in the road," so to speak, we are driven by what is best for us instead of what is right. Our biased perception can cause us to ignore reality and not foresee the consequences. We all encounter tough decisions, and what makes them tougher are the "blind spots" in the road that don't allow us to see what will ultimately come as a result of our choices. For some it may be betraying a friend, while for others it may be distorting a written policy to fit our current desires. At times it may be as simple as being late for a scheduled event because of weather conditions that made the roads treacherous.

Let's back up. The morning you are late to this event isn't due to the road conditions; it is due to you choosing not to set the alarm an hour earlier when you knew it was snowing as you went to bed. *You* made the choice. People who arrived at the event on time followed the directions and made a choice to be on time. However, our biased perception tells us that we won't get in trouble for being late, and other people will be late, thus blinding us to the truth. We offer excuses and often don't acknowledge or take ownership for the situation. What could have been avoided isn't, and any consequences are a result of our choice to waiver from the directions. What throws us off course, and takes the enjoyment out of the trip, is when we stray from the directions. The media is filled with stories from businesses that fail to marriages that crumble, because someone chose not to follow the directions. Maybe a good question at this point would be, "How do you prepare to make the right turn when you arrive at a fork in the road?" First and foremost, you have to acquire the essential quality of discipline.

Discipline is doing what you really
don't want to do so you can do what you really
want to do.

You cannot be successful in your personal and professional endeavors without discipline. You must be able to pay the price in little things so you can receive the bigger things – or, as my Mom used to say, "Be able to give up the good things in life so you can someday have the best things." So many relationships fail because people aren't willing to pay the price and make the sacrifices. You give in to your weakness and forever go around lamenting, "If I had only..." You must be able to face up to your weaknesses. As long as they remain, they will hinder and keep you from maximum success and, most importantly, the inner peace you are searching for.

Take a moment to identify five things about yourself that you believe you need to strengthen to maximize your success and to reach your personal and professional goals. A good example for me was the people I used to surround myself with. Being raised in a Christian home, I was always influenced to do right and make the right choices. As I grew older I began to acquire friends who didn't have the same beliefs or values that I had. Soon I began to struggle with my choices and many times didn't have the discipline to make the right decisions. It was only then I realized that in order to be the person I wanted to be, I had to surround myself with the character of people who resembled whom I wanted to become. Because we are what we repeatedly do, we can find ourselves beginning to do things that at the time seem harmless, yet the repercussions can be detrimental. Here is some good advice I learned from my mother. Never put yourself in a situation that would allow you to compromise what you believe. When you are married, never permit yourself to be one-on-one with the opposite gender even if it is an innocent setting. Your intent, based on your values, isn't in question, but their intent, based on their values, may be something you live to regret. The innocence of circumstances and the naivety of intentions are no match for the impact of the result. So how do you develop this discipline? First, use your head, or, a modern way of saying it, refine your thinking. Use the mind that God has given you to think about the right things and those things that are pure. Pure and positive thoughts lead to pure and positive actions. You also must master your emotions or be mastered by them. You don't turn off your feelings; however, you shouldn't let your feelings prevent you from doing what is right. People overeat, drink excessively, or seek another release because of their inability to acquire disciplined emotions. The key to mastering any problem is to master *you.*

The mastery of life is the mastery of self.

To become more disciplined, you will have to understand what affects your decisions on an everyday basis. All of these decisions when connected put you on a course that defines your ultimate life path.

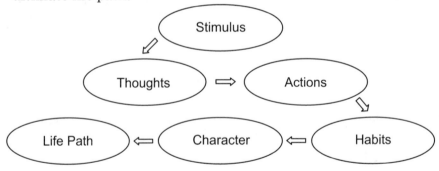

It begins with stimulus, or the plural of the word, *stimuli.* Stimulus is anything that rouses, incites, or spurs you on. It is an incentive that causes you to change an activity. It is also either positive or negative. The two main sources of stimuli are information and people. The great thing about these sources is that you have the ability to choose them. Every day when you wake up, you begin choosing the information you will take in. For some it is the television, while for others it may be the newspaper, yet others may choose to spend time reading a good book. So if you are a person who is hooked on watching and reading the news, what kind of stimulus would you describe it as? Maybe I should ask it this way: What do all the negative events of the world rouse, incite, and spur you on to do? If you are a person who enjoys watching soap operas, what stimulus does that produce? Think about this: If a sixty-second commercial can sell you a product (one sixty-second 2003 Super Bowl ad at $4.4 million), then what do you think a sixty-minute program can sell you? It can sell you a lifestyle or a slanted manner of thinking. Remember, as stated earlier, discipline requires you to refine your thinking. And what about the people you choose to associate with every day? Are they positive? Do they share your same values? Do they respect you for who you are and what you believe? Would they turn right at the fork in the road or, when given a chance, would they deceive you to get what they want?

---

*Your mind will give back exactly what
you put into it.*

I am always hurt, but never amazed, when I hear of the tragic breakup of certain couples. In most cases, one or both partners begin to take in the wrong information, or allow themselves to associate with the wrong people. They are guided by their emotions and, sadly, begin to listen to those who don't share their values but pose as friends who empathize with their circumstances. Soon they are trapped, because the stimuli of misinformation and charming people produce their *thoughts.*

These thoughts are a direct result of the information and people they are now allowing to infiltrate their thoughts. They begin trusting these people and relying on them for their direction, never realizing that danger is lurking within because they abandon what they believe. Their thought process begins to rationalize behavior, and before they realize it, the thoughts have produced *actions*. The actions may be innocent reactions to your thoughts, but as they perpetuate, they become knowingly a part of your new behavior patterns. Your fulfillment is temporary, and soon you begin to recognize that your unbridled release is a result of underlying emotions. This release may begin as an emotional affair when communicating with someone, but, tragically, it turns into something regrettable and inerasable. When repeated often enough, your actions become *habits*.

I am your constant companion. I will push you on or drag you down to failure. I am completely at your command. Half the things you do might just as well be turned over to me, and I will be able to do them quickly and correctly. I am easily managed; you must merely be firm with me. Show me exactly how you want something done and after a few lessons I will do it automatically. I am the servant of all great people, and, alas, of all failures as well. Those who are great I have made great. Those who are failures I have made failures. I am not a machine, though I work with the precision of a machine plus the intelligence of a person. You may run me for profit or run me for ruin; it makes no difference to me. Take me, train me, be firm with me, and I will place the world at your feet. Be easy with me and I will destroy you. Who am I? I am your habits.

Your habits are what make up your *character*. Your character will be determined by what you stand for, fall for, and lie for. A lack of character is a direct result of your lack of discipline. Discipline is doing the right things at the right time for the right reason. How are you doing when it comes to discipline? Do you sometimes regret that you've been unable to get yourself to do what is right? Unless you change your stimuli, which produce your thoughts, your actions will become habits that erode your character, which ultimately produces your *life path*. Every person who has ever fallen victim to an affair can trace its origin to the stimuli permitted prior to it happening. Your acquisition of discipline and the monitoring of your stimuli can help you make the right choices; however, the real key is your willingness to grow.

Human growth is a process of arriving at the fork in the road and, through experimentation, trial, and error, ultimately leading to wisdom.

Each time you are faced with a choice – your arrival at the fork in the road – trust yourself and take action. Your bad choices are no less valuable than your good choices, depending on how you learn from them. Perceived failures usually provide more learning than perceived successes. When you fail at something – marriage, child rearing, business, friendship, or whatever your perceived failure is – your first reaction is to feel that you have failed. While it is easy to jump to this depressing conclusion, it will impede your ability to grow and enjoy the ride more later down the road. Every fork in the road where you make the wrong turn is a chance to learn something new and grow from the experience. The pain and suffering usually cloud your ability to have compassion towards yourself and continue trusting your decisions. Compassion will open the door of forgiveness and will allow you to avoid a continuation of self-critical thoughts. You need to begin practicing compassion so it can break down the barriers that allow you to connect with yourself and others. The Bible is a great place to start – "We have all sinned and come short of His glory." The key to learning the lesson of compassion is realizing that you are in control of the erection or destruction of those barriers that create distance between you and others. You can choose to dissolve those barriers when you want to connect with the heart of another human being. You judge yourself and others, and it limits and prevents you from being compassionate when and where that is needed. You put yourself into a box of self-righteousness and even go so far as to compare your errors in judgment to someone else's. You say, "I'm not as bad as they are" and "I didn't see the harm," and condone your poor judgment, cutting yourself off from your need to connect with other people. You may feel superior to those you are judging, but you may also feel the chill of your loneliness imposed by your isolation.

Compassion opens limitless doors to human connection.

My oldest son, Stephen, is a great example of someone who arrived at the fork in the road and turned left. During his freshman year in college, he was arrested for possessing marijuana. Lacking the discipline necessary to make the right choice, he found himself saying, "My life is over," at the tender age of 19. But through a series of counseling sessions, a lot of prayer, and his ability to forgive himself, he is now stronger at age 23 than he has ever been. His growth has been tremendous, and his influence on others is even more powerful. His secret? Changing his stimuli, becoming more disciplined, and eliminating his destructive habits. His college roommate, fraternity friends, and misinformation caused a chain reaction that began with his thoughts, which produced a set of actions, and ended up in a habit that eventually got him arrested. Today his friends are different, his information intake has changed, his thought process is different, and most of all, he has mastered his emotions.

During the fourteenth century there lived a man named Raynald III. Raynald was a nobleman, the rightful duke over his ancestral lands, but his younger brother revolted against him and surpassed him. Raynald's brother needed the duke out of the way, but he didn't want to kill him, so he came up with an ingenious plan. Because Raynald was a very large man, his brother had put him into a room with a smaller-than-average door. If Raynald would simply lose some weight, he would be allowed to leave. In fact, the usurping brother promised that if Raynald left the room, his freedom and his rule would be restored. But Raynald was not a man of discipline, and his brother knew that. Every day the brother had trays of delicious food delivered to his older brother's room. And Raynald ate. In fact, instead of growing thinner, he grew fatter and fatter.

A person lacking discipline and unwilling to grow is in a prison without bars. Are your lack of discipline and destructive habits making you turn left at the fork in the road? Unleash the power within you to make the right choices and start enjoying the ride.

REMEMBER THE RAINBOW

No One Can Ruin Your Trip
Without Your Permission

---

*Adversity will help you decide what you
really believe.*

On a recent flight from Atlanta, Georgia, to San Francisco, California, approximately twenty minutes prior to landing the pilot announced that we were about to "experience some rough air and the ride might get a little bumpy." True to his word, because of a storm in the Bay Area, the ride became extremely rough. After we landed, the gentleman who had been sitting next to me prompted me to look out the window at what he and I both described as one of the most magnificent rainbows we have ever seen. He then said, "I guess the rough ride was worth it." His point was made and again reminded me that we have to put up with a little rain some days in order to see the rainbow. Unfortunately, opportunity always looks bigger going than coming. Our children, relationships, and professional endeavors have a sprinkling of rain and, in some cases, storms that seemingly will never end; however, our reaction to them always determines the outcome. Personally, I never thought I would survive the biggest storm of my life a few years ago, yet my mother continuously kept me focused on the rainbow. The remarkable part of life is that we all have a choice when it comes to our attitude and outlook on life. People blame so much of their attitude on circumstances without taking responsibility for how they react to them.

Life picks on everyone...don't take it personally.

Fumbling is part of football, failing is part of succeeding, and hurting is part of loving. Every situation in life is our perception to it, not the reality of it. The glass is half empty or half full, and sometimes our perception will be based on whether we're pouring or drinking. True to form, as in most circumstances, just as the biggest storm of my life was ending I suddenly looked up one day and saw the rainbow – the greatest gift God ever gave me, my loving sons, Stephen and Josh.

As stated in previous chapters, it is important to understand what changes you can make to remember the rainbow. First, I want you to think about three things that you really enjoy doing. Next, think about three things you really don't enjoy doing. What is common to those things you enjoy doing? What is common to those things you don't enjoy doing? My guess is that you will discover that the things you enjoy doing are the ones you get to choose, while the things you really don't enjoy are the ones that leave you no choice. Dancing, reading, and singing karaoke are some things you may enjoy and you can choose; however, laundry, cleaning, and grocery shopping are "must do's" with little or no choice. The next thing you will discover is that the "enjoy" list has rewards, while the "don't enjoy" list is non-rewarding and never-ending. What is the reward for grocery shopping? You get to put the groceries away. And which of your two lists do you control? Which of your two lists is self-assessment instead of outside assessment? If singing is on your "enjoy" list, that is total self-assessment. You choose to sing in the car and your assessment isn't critical but rather self-pleasing. On the other hand, when you consider cleaning, it is an endless task, and the assessment process is readily apparent when people visit your house. The "don't enjoy" list can cause you stress, while the "enjoy" list is relaxing. A great example of an activity that can cause some people to relax while others might stress is the working of a crossword puzzle. If it is on your "enjoy" list, you approach it with excitement and firmly believe you will solve it. When it is on your "don't enjoy" list, your approach is different and your mindset in solving it becomes one of futility and hopelessness. Even in something this simple, our attitude determines our approach, which is precisely what happens in life.

Our attitude determines our approach to life.

Look around you. Analyze the conversations of people who lead unhappy, unfulfilled lives. You will find that they are crying out against society, which they feel is out to give them a lifetime of trouble, misery, and bad luck.

Sometimes the prison of discontent has been built by our own hands. The world doesn't care whether we free ourselves from the prison or not. Adopting a good, healthy attitude toward life does not affect society nearly as much as it affects us. It would be impossible to estimate the number of jobs that have been lost, the number of promotions missed, the number of sales not made, and the number of marriages ruined by poor attitudes. But almost daily we witness jobs that are held but hated and marriages that are tolerated but unhappy, all because people are waiting for others, or the world, to change instead of realizing that they are responsible for their behavior. Your situations will never be all tailor-made to fit you perfectly, but your attitudes can tailor-make the situation.

Most days you will not get what you want; some days you will only get what you need; but every day you will get what you expect.

Our attitude also determines our relationship with people. If you are a Christian, this statement should take on even more meaning since our effectiveness and ministry are based on relationships. Yet establishing fulfilling relationships is difficult. People we live beside, work with, attend church with, and even live with can differ in values, vision, and outlook. While you may remember the rainbow and see the best in most situations, others may see the world through a window of cynicism and regret. The key is making sure your attitude is an example of what you value and believe in.

Nothing is as contagious as example.

Your relationship with people is determined by how closely you align with their values or how much they reflect something you love or hate about yourself. People are drawn to individuals who stand for something and have a clear view of right and wrong. They are even more attracted to people who display an attitude of optimism, who don't overreact to situations, and who walk the message that they talk. Consider the passage way created by two people who are drawn together and then discover that their values and attitudes are in alignment. If your belief is that family is the basis of a healthy life, and if your values include spending time with family, then your behaviors will include meals together, weekends and vacations together, and the like. So stop reading, take a moment and ask yourself, Would my attitude, outlook, and values attract people to me or repel them from me? Your attitude is either your best friend or your worst enemy. Your reactions to other people, however, are really just barometers for how you perceive yourself. Your reactions to others say more about you than they do about others. We are usually drawn to those who are most like us and tend to dislike those who display those aspects of ourselves that we dislike. Hence, to find the rainbow in some relationships you must practice the art of tolerance. Tolerance is when you learn to embrace all parts of others and allow them to express themselves fully as the unique human beings they are.

I am completely convinced that I now enjoy the ride so much more because I stopped judging everyone else so harshly in order to feel good about myself. In my own mind, my intolerance of them rendered me superior. When you judge other people harshly, it is your way of covering up feelings of insufficiency and insecurity. I remember attending a church for several years where most of the members would sit in the same seats virtually every Sunday. I was no exception. Every Sunday I would sit in my same pew behind two ladies who always arrived earlier than most so they could fellowship (gossip) prior to worship service. When I look back on that experience, I can't help but remember some of their comments as people entered the sanctuary: "He wore that suit last Sunday. You would think he would have enough pride in himself to wear something different." "If she knew what she looked like in that dress from behind she would never wear it again." "That skirt is way too short for church. That is an abomination...I would never."

Before I began enjoying the ride, I would rarely allow myself to relate to anyone who was not exactly like me. Today I find my ride more enriching because I use my judgments to learn more about myself. I have discovered that although I am different from so many people, it doesn't make them wrong nor does it make me wrong; it simply makes us who we are.

You are everything you choose to be.

When the storms of life come and you begin to run for cover, your lifelong programming will take over and the end results will be a matter of your own thought process. The Bible has a familiar passage which reads, "So as a man thinketh." This Biblical passage hits the nail right on the head. The human brain, that incredibly powerful personal computer that each of us has, is capable of doing so much *for* us or so much *against* us. If you give your mental computer the wrong directions, it will act on those wrong directions. Those of you with children might want to pay extra attention to this particular portion of this chapter. During the first eighteen years of our lives, if we grew up in average, reasonably positive homes, we were told no, or what we could *not* do, more than 148,000 times. Meanwhile, during that same period of time, how many times were you told what you *could* do or what you could accomplish? This negative programming that we all received, and still receive, has come to us unintentionally. It has come from our parents, who just wanted to protect us; from our brothers and sisters, our teachers, our schoolmates, our associates at work, our life mates, advertising of all kinds, the morning paper, and the six o'clock news. As I stated earlier, your mind will give back exactly what you put into it. Behavioral researchers estimate that as much as seventy-seven percent of everything we think is negative, counterproductive, and works against us. Your brain simply believes what you tell it the most. And what you tell it about you, it will create. It has no choice.

Some people never remember, or tragically never see, the rainbows because they have been programmed not to. What if each and every day, from the time you were a small child, you had been given an extra helping of self-confidence, double the amount of determination, and twice the amount of belief in the outcome? Can you imagine what tasks you might have accomplished more easily, what problems you might have overcome, or what goals you might have reached? After all, success, ultimately, is up to the individual. It isn't the pen; it's the writer. It isn't the road; it's the runner.

I remember being introduced on a radio talk show as a motivational speaker and an author in the field of motivation. The interviewer's first question was, "Steve, are you one of those guys that gets people jumping in the aisles, walking on hot coals, and ready to run out and conquer the world?" I know my answer surprised him. My response was, "No!" In fact, I'm very skeptical when people give three or four habits, steps, or strategies to people and assure them that if followed they will stay motivated. Most motivation is like a bowl of cereal – it just doesn't last long and you end up hungry in a few hours. As a speaker and author I firmly believe my primary purpose is to get a person thinking. When I can penetrate a person's heart through their mind, I have found the ultimate source of their motivation. Motivation is an inside job that is determined by the individual person. When they discover something about themselves they need to change, they make the decision, not I. By painting pictures and using real life examples, I challenge a person to take a good hard look at where they are and where they would like to end up. I also make sure that my approach is realistic and within reach, but even then I remind myself that I provide external motivation that does not last unless the internal programming permits it.

The greatest thing you will ever learn is to use it.

Numerous times I have people come up to me and say, "I really enjoyed your seminar and got so much out of it."

My response is simple: "How will you use it?" To have people run out of a seminar with good intentions is exciting. To have people run out of a seminar with an internal action plan is life changing. I am always amazed at some players on sports teams that rely on the coach to motivate them. Great teams have individual players who are self-motivated. If it takes another person to motivate you, then you will always live your life with a multitude of peaks and valleys. The same principle is apparent when people are looking for happiness. If you are seeking to find a person who can make you happy, then you will never find happiness.

If you find yourself having several bad days mixed in with your good days, stop giving people and circumstances permission to ruin your days. Road rage is something I understand but have trouble comprehending. To have a total stranger pull out in front of you at a stop sign, and you get angry and give them an obscene gesture is incomprehensible. I understand your frustration, but fail to see why you would allow that incident to have any bearing on the rest of your day, if only for a moment. Express lines at grocery stores are another great example of where you permit someone else to dictate your day. You stand frustrated, even angry, with a total stranger who ignores the "Ten items or less" sign. Have you ever been in a store where they have an "express line security person" counting the items in everyone's cart? Since there are no such people, it is better to spend your time focused on something else that will allow you to remember the rainbow. I never leave home without a book, or at a checkout counter I "borrow" a magazine to pass the time and keep me positively focused. You leave for the store, come home in a mood, and blame someone else for it.

One exercise I always employ to keep me focused, positive, and happy is the remembrances of my own children, my own happy childhood memories, or the actions of other children present. The innocence of a child can quickly blow the storm clouds away and allow you to see the brilliance of the rainbow. I remember when my sons were growing up and they were afraid to sleep in their own beds because of the fear of darkness. Night after night they would crawl in, one by one, with my wife and me. I tried everything to rid them, and me, of this pesky problem. I bribed them, chased the "boogie men" away, and even rewarded them if they stayed in their own beds. On one occasion, when I was leaving for a trip, I promised them a nice present when I returned home if they slept in their own bed and not Mommy's. On my return trip, I invited my boss to join me for dinner, and he would ride from the airport with me and I would carry him home instead of his wife having to pick him up. Upon our arrival at my house, no sooner did we open the car doors than my sons came running out of the house and down the driveway to meet us. All excited and out of breath, my youngest son, Josh, said, "Dad, did you bring us our present?" I told him I did, to which he said, "You are going to be so happy, Dad; while you were gone on this trip, nobody slept with Mommy." Every time I get preoccupied or caught up with something life is tossing at me, the only way I can get by it and move on is to remember "this too shall pass" and keep my head up so I don't miss the colors of the rainbow.

DARE TO BE DIFFERENT

Comparison Prohibits You From Seeing Your Uniqueness

Never be content with someone else's
definition of you.

The new millennium ushered in the catchphrases "Think outside the box," "Color outside the lines," and "First break all the rules." For many people, these were nothing more than cute slogans intended to challenge them to be more creative. For others, it was a removal of their constant fear of failure. Anything worth doing requires some risk, and with risk comes failure. Federal Express rocked the world in the '70s with its door-to-door service, and Southwest Airlines questioned and challenged decades of conventional wisdom. So what about you? Are you constantly comparing yourself to someone else? Do you own your expectations, or have you inherited someone else's? Do you own mistakes, share mistakes, learn from mistakes, and then move on? Regardless of your answers, the fact remains that you can enjoy the trip so much more if you stop focusing on someone else's definition of you.

Federal Express and Southwest Airlines are excellent examples of organizations that created their own reality and dared to be different. The ride you take in this lifetime will be so much more rewarding if you define your own worth and just be who God intended you to be. Some people spend a lifetime living a lie and enduring their existence rather than untying themselves from things they can't control. They pity and belittle themselves, take things personally, and let everyone else decide their worth. Authorship of your life is one of your absolute rights. You have all the tools and resources you need. What you do with them is up to you. Your life has the potential to be a wondrous journey if you are open to explore all that is available to you. Imagine yourself at 90 years old, looking back at your life. What do you want to see, a life filled with regrets because you never had complete self-acceptance that would allow you to fully participate in all aspects of life?

To laugh is human, at yourself is divine.

On a recent trip to New York I ventured off Broadway to see a play entitled *I Love You, You're Perfect, Now Change.* The storyline of the play was about relationships. You meet a person, tell them how perfect they are, profess your love, call them your soul mate, and then proceed to try and change everything about them that you don't like. People see us one way, we see ourselves a different way, and in reality the view from each perspective, although different, isn't a true view of who we really are. Singer Michael Jackson is a great example of someone who allows so many other people to define who he is. He is known for his creative genius regarding music, yet what draws the most attention is his sordid saga of plastic surgery, baby dangling, and bed sharing. He spent millions to change his appearance, and now he spends millions to defend it. Sad, but true; Michael Jackson distinguished himself through his music yet allowed other people to determine his self-worth through his appearance. Sound familiar? I meet people every day who bemoan something about themselves that binds them from becoming the person God intended them to be. We see them, they see themselves, and yet because of their inability to be who they really are, we never really get to know them, and, unfortunately, they live their lives pretending to be something they are not.

No one can make you feel inferior without
your consent.

Where do your feelings of worthiness stem from? Self-esteem is feeling worthy and able to meet life's challenges. It is the essence from which we measure our worth and the most important building blocks in the foundation of accepting yourself for who you are. Your body may teach you the lesson of self-esteem by testing your willingness to view yourself as worthy, regardless of what you look like or how your body performs. The process of building self-esteem is to identify what stands in your way and then take action to make a positive change. What stands in your way the most is usually your inability to change what is most important – your inner self. I have known people who wanted nothing more than to fix a problem at home or at work, or wanted to change some small things about themselves or in their lives that would help them grow or make life a little easier. I have also known people who were fed up with everything. They wanted to change their lives in a major way – different job, new husband or wife, sell out and move to another state – they wanted to do whatever it would take to change their lives and change their futures. I have known people who tried to change their lives by changing their homes, cars, or careers. But for most of them the change wasn't a real change; it didn't work. They took their old selves with them. Changes of heart are as fragile and as temporary as changes of costumes in a play. We can change friends, spouses, jobs, or locations, and we will still take the same inner selves along with us – the same internal identities that made us unhappy, helped us, or got us into trouble in the first place. If we take the old images of ourselves with us wherever we go and into whatever we do, how could we expect to do better the next time?

The mastery of life is the mastery of self.

If you want to be real and who you really are, then at the outset decide who is in command and who or what is in control of your life. When you let someone else, or something else, decide your worth and your destiny, chances are you will never master yourself. Change occurs either as a result of something outside of you that happens *to you*, or as a result of something within you that causes the changes to take place.

The kind of change that happens *to us* is a result of those minor attitude changes which come to us by way of expectations, minor events, company policies, personal relationships, relatives, family needs, parental authority, religious credos, peer pressures, advertising of all kinds, economic trends, daily exposure to television, radio, magazines and newspapers, social requirements, political positions, whimsical notions, close friends, and off-hand comments.

It is strange that these influences should shape most of our lives for us, yet they do. They are not all bad or contrary, of course – some are necessary and worthwhile. Some of these influences, a few of them, are the best we can hope to find. But once again, the choice is yours and no one else's. Who you are, where you are heading, and what you become should solely rest on you and not the pressure applied by someone else.

The conditioning of *daily living* somehow convinces you that your greatest need, social survival, is also your greatest achievement. The result is that we slowly, unknowingly change, not to achieve but to survive, in a way that offers acceptance of others. We get by. We do what we must. We do as well as we can, get along with others as well as possible, play our roles, do our jobs, put away a little for the future, and hope for the best.

The dreams we dreamed as children we learn no longer to believe, because we dare to be different.

That is the tune we are taught to play. Instead of believing, knowing, that each of us is an entire orchestra, we are led to believe we are only the flute. We listen to idle gossip of a friend, follow the lead of so-called leaders, fit our lives into a mold that was not of our making, tuck our dreams into our pockets, and hope for better things to come.

I can still remember my days in high school like they were yesterday. If you were an athlete or a cheerleader, your future looked bright and your social presence was rewarding. If you were into computers – remember, this was the '70s – you were as "geeky" as those who aspired to perform in the school band. A friend of mine named Justin was into acting and was forever teased about his role as a thespian in our high school. He would never go on to pursue his love of acting and eventually ended up working in a department store in our hometown. Do you think anyone ever told Fred Astaire he couldn't dance or act when he was growing up? They did. As a matter of fact, after his first screen test it was written, "He can't act, can dance a little, and is slightly balding." Decca Records told a musical group that guitars were on their way out and their hair was too long. The great thing about the Beatles is that they determined their own worth, decided to be different, and proved to Decca and the world that being different doesn't make you wrong; it just makes you different. After a tryout, a young kid from Mississippi was told by the director of talent at the Grand Ole Opry that he should go back home and continue driving a truck. Because I am such a big fan, I am so glad Elvis was okay with being different. And so we are changed by the lives we live. For most of us it is seldom the calamitous change of catastrophic events. It is the slow, sure change of environment – the change forced upon us by the world around us. What we become a part of becomes a part of us. What we perceive and accept is an important part of what we, too, will become.

What you decide to do next will determine what you do next.

What you do, how you live, what you become, is almost entirely up to you. Make the decision to do what you choose, and your next step will be your own. Sit back and let the outside world influence and take the lead and it will. Decide to determine your own next step – and thereby your future – and you can. Make the decision to make each breath you breathe your own. Stick by it, and each breath, step, motion, and achievement will be of your own making and your own choice.

Just as the thoughts, ideas, demands, and influences of others have guided, controlled, and directed most of our lives in the past, it is the personal control of our own minds that now gives us a chance to change our futures – for ourselves. You can do so much. You can, if you choose, break through the wall that stands between you and anything you would like to change or achieve. Give yourself the will to do it. Give yourself the belief, the attitude, the emotion, and the action that will get you where you want to be.

Your greatest adversary in being yourself is yourself. It is your own thinking which has created the limited self-portraits of whom you believed yourself to be. So much energy is displaced on being someone or something else that the resourcefulness necessary to being you is never accomplished. People who live double lives are victim to the endless entanglement of wanting one thing while portraying something else. My mother used to call it "wanting my cake and eating it too." The sooner you realize that the grass *is* sometimes greener on the other side, but someday you will have to cut it, fertilize it, and weed it, the sooner you will start leading *your* life.

Revealing of feelings is the beginning of healing.

Earlier I stated that being different doesn't make you wrong; it just makes you different. Interestingly enough, some people believe that the reason they have so many problems is because of who they are; thus they try to be different to avoid the problems. As irrational as it sounds, people sometimes fear being themselves, because they perceive themselves as being more problematic than what they try to be. Here are four things that should help you understand better and make you focus more on being you than trying to be someone else.

First realize that everybody faces problems. No matter how far you go or how successful you become, you will continue to face difficulties. The Barna Research Group surveyed more than twelve hundred people to gather information on problems they faced. They were asked to identify their single most serious need or problem. Here are their answers, along with the percentage of people who ranked the problems most pressing:

39% Financial
16% Job-Related
12% Personal Health
8% Time and Stress
7% Parenting
6% Educational Attainment
3% Fear of Crime
3% Personal Relationships

As you can see, people face a variety of problems, with money being the greatest. And I am sure that some of you reading this book have said, "If I only made more money, I wouldn't have the problems I have." Which brings us to number two: Money doesn't solve problems. The opposite is actually true – people with money tend to be less content and have additional problems. A larger percentage of the rich have drug and alcohol problems than the general population. They try to escape themselves by purchasing things that they feel can make them happy or content. The bottom line is that money is no substitute for solving your problems, and financial problems are usually a symptom of other personal problems.

Another common misconception is that successful people have achieved because they didn't have problems. But that isn't true. Not only do people overcome obstacles to become successful, but even after they have achieved a level of success they continue to face problems. The fact is, the higher people go – personally and professionally – the more complicated life gets. Schedules get tighter, money issues increase, and greater demands are put on successful people. But do they change who they are and what they believe in, or do they continue being who they are by growing and developing themselves and increasing their ability to deal with problems?

To thoroughly enjoy the ride you must first learn that you can't make the trip in a day.

The final thing necessary to help you be yourself is to realize that problems provide an opportunity for growth. Ask yourself this question: When was the last time I really grew as an individual? Was it during your vacation, a cruise, a sporting event, or some other fun and entertaining event? Or could it have been when you were struggling through something? Chances are most of you identified your biggest growth during a time that challenged you the most. For some of you maturity, completeness, and contentment are at stake when you face problems. To grow into the real you, understand what you must do with your problems. Realize their purpose, recognize your dependence, and risk disclosure. The moment this happens, it will help you grow, draw closer to God, and, most importantly, display your authenticity. Today is the day to give yourself the greatest gift you will ever give – who you really are!

REFOCUS YOUR ATTENTION

Decide What's Important and Never Take It for Granted

Never let the urgent get in the way of the important.

In October of 2001, I was speaking to a group of six hundred people in Los Angeles, California, and asked them to raise their hand in response to this statement: "If you have children at home and/or are married with your spouse living at home, please raise your hand." Virtually every hand was in the air. Later that morning I would ask them this question: "How many of you believe that the tragic events of September 11, 2001, were a wake-up call?" To this question I wasn't surprised to see the large crowd almost unanimously raise their hand. What did surprise me was their response to my next immediate question: "How many of you this morning spent at least five minutes sitting at breakfast with your children and/or your spouse?" Then, "How many of you left this morning for this event and, prior to leaving, kissed your children, regardless of their age, and/or your spouse and told them how much you loved them?" To the first question only seventeen people raised their hands, to the latter question only about fifty in the entire room. The events of 9/11 helped us to refocus our attention, but for too many it was only temporary. You profess to the world what is so important to you, then proceed to live your day taking it for granted so many times. The urgency of career, social events, material possessions, non-family relationships, television, and the Internet take precedence over what is most important.

At this point in the book, I want you to mark your place and go retrieve something to write with and something to write on. Now that you have your paper and writing utensil, I want you to make a list of everything that is important in your life. Don't hurry, and be sure to be exhaustive in your thought process. You may want to make the list one day and then revisit it the next day to be sure you haven't forgotten anything or anyone. After you have your list completed, then narrow it down to the five most important things in your life. Be sure to only list five. Once you have determined the five most important things in your life, put those five things in order of importance. The first time I did this exercise, my list looked liked this:

1. Relationship with God
2. Stephen and Josh
3. Mother
4. Health
5. Family and friends

Your list doesn't have to match mine; your list is *your* list. Now that you have determined the five most important things in your life, it is time to see if your actions match your list. Write down the number 168 on the top of your paper. This number represents the last seven days times twenty-four hours that you have spent on this earth. Look at your list and write down how much time you have spent on, or with, the five most important things in your life.

Love doesn't make the world go around,
but it sure makes the trip a whole lot
more exciting.

Caution: You can't count the time as time spent when you are in a room with someone and the television is on. Nor can you count the time when you are in a car and the radio is on. If specific people are on your list, you may only count the time you have spent with them either one-on-one or focused completely on them as a whole. My guess is that for many of you this will be an incredible revelation, and you may realize that you, too, have taken what is important for granted too many times.

When I assigned a time to my list, it came out looking like this:

> Relationship with God – 1 hour
> Stephen and Josh – 3 hours
> Mother – 1 hour
> Health – 1 hour
> Family and friends – 1 hour

Can you imagine? I spent 7 out of 168 possible hours in a week on the five most important things in my life. You should remember reading at the beginning of this chapter, "Never let the urgent get in the way of what is important." Too many times we profess to the world what is of utmost importance to us, yet our actions tell a different story. Career, social events, non-family relationships, television, and the Internet monopolize our time, and before we know it, we focus on the wrong thing. I am not suggesting you quit your job and go on welfare to spend more time with your family, but what I am suggesting is that you realize today, before it is too late, that the ride you are taking will only be as rewarding as the time you have spent focused on what is important. I have never met a dying person who said, "I wish I had spent more time at the office." But I have met people who spent their last days on earth apologizing for not spending enough time doing what was important. We all have a tendency to lose focus and get caught up in the excitement of what the world now offers. Stop wasting your time trying to keep up with the Joneses. Just bring them down to your level – it's cheaper!

Life provides every opportunity to get it right.

Perhaps you are reading this, looking back and asking yourself, "What if … ?" Beware of unanswered questions! Where you have been and what you have done make you who you are. To sit around and continually wonder what might have been only serves to defeat your future purpose of what can be. I have talked with men who never spent time with their children and lamented about missing them grow up, yet they continue to miss the next stages of their lives because they focus on what they didn't do instead of what they could be doing. Children are very resilient; however, as they grow older, their naivety towards life changes, and the impressions we make start to imprint them either negatively or positively. It is never too late to refocus your attention; however, your ability to forgive yourself may overtake the drive to begin anew and focus on what really matters. When we begin thinking back, two things will always come to the forefront – resentment and regret. When we are dealing with resentment from the past, our thoughts are directed towards another person. Our energy is displaced on something negative, non-urgent, and non-important. Likewise, our regrets consume so much negative energy and they, too, are non-urgent, non-important, and non-productive. However, your regrets are not about another person; they are about you. Either way, you spend precious time focused on things that are not important and non-rewarding.

I recently caught myself reminiscing about when my youngest son, Josh, played high school sports. I remember his sophomore year like it was yesterday. He lettered in football, basketball, and baseball, but instead of being the proud father, I caught myself cursing the times I had to run him back and forth from one practice to another. Yet on Senior Night, during his final year as an athlete, I remember his words to me as we walked onto the football field in front of a crowded stadium. He said, "Dad, I just wanted to say thanks for all the times you took me to practice. You're one of the only parents who never complained about it, and I just wanted to say thanks." Embarrassed, I stood in tears, realizing it would be the last time I ever stood on that field with either of my sons. I began to think about the times I got frustrated when it came time to pick him up, and how I would give almost anything to do it again. Time goes by so fast and we are so wrapped up in what is seemingly so urgent that before we know it they are off to college, get married, have children, and see you during the holidays if you're lucky. The song that became famous in 1974, "Cat's in the Cradle," said it all: "A child arrived just the other day...and now he's driving!"

Time is irreversible and irreplaceable.

After you decide what is important and commit to never taking it for granted, the key will be balance – *internal* and *external*. The thing you must balance internally is your *mental well-being, emotional well-being, physical well-being,* and *spiritual well-being.* Your external balance consists of *family, work, play, relationships, social life,* your *financial well-being,* and your *activities.* Wow! Too often you will catch yourself focusing so much of your energies on two or three things while depriving yourself of the necessary ingredients to being a whole person – someone who has achieved inner peace. Take a look at your life from a whole-person perspective and evaluate which parts are in balance and which parts may be out of balance. With one being the lowest and ten being the highest, how would you rate your balance in each of the ten areas previously mentioned? So where do you spend most of your day?

Ask yourself these life-balancing questions: What part of your internal balance needs improvement? Do you daily feed each of these areas, or do you neglect one while focusing entirely on another? Do you permit someone else to rob you of feeding your internal balancers? For example, is someone daily robbing you of the emotional well-being that you deserve, which is so vital to your inner peace? If so, you need to renegotiate your relationships and begin feeding your emotional self with positive influences. All too often the person you forget in the equation for happiness is yourself. When you list all the important things in your life, make sure you are on the list. If you spend so much time focused on everyone else, you may find yourself at a crossroads, struggling for peace and contentment, only realizing the life you are living is based on everyone else but yourself. Your emotional, physical, spiritual, and mental well-being are just as important as the external areas that will require your attention. Your family is extremely important, and I am sure family will show up on your top five list of important things; however, too much time spent with family while being stingy with several other external balancers will cause tension, stress, and irritability. When you catch yourself being cranky or short, review the list of external balancers and internal balancers and see where you are falling short. The benefits of achieving balance in your life are many. First and foremost it will cultivate richer relationships. As mentioned earlier, relationships are an intricate and necessary part of your life. Of the three resources you have available, people are the only unlimited resource you have. Science has proved you will also live longer. Researchers at Mayo Clinic, reporting on a study that spanned three decades, said they have found that optimistic people live about 19 percent longer than pessimists. "It confirmed our common sense belief," said Toshihiko Maruta, a psychiatrist who was the lead researcher in the project. "It tells us that mind and body are linked and that attitude has an impact on the final outcome — death."

And then there is happiness. Happiness comes from within. It consists of not having, but of being; not of possessing, but of enjoying. It is one of the incidental by-products of an unselfish life. The basis of happiness is the love of something outside of self. Unhappiness is the hunger to get; happiness is the hunger to give. If the individual should set out for a single day to give happiness, to make life happier, brighter and sweeter, not for him, but for others, he would find a wondrous revelation of what happiness really is. We cannot tell what may happen to us in the strange medley of life, but we can decide what happens in us, how we can take it, what we can do with it. But maybe the most important life-balancing benefit is inner peace. As mentioned earlier in the book, achieving inner peace involves making good decisions and setting the right priorities. It comes from building lasting, genuine, healthy relationships. It comes from making genuine, permanent commitments in marriage and forming lasting, unconditional relationships with your kids, your loved ones, and your friends

---

The most precious things in life cannot be built by hand or bought by man.

A group of students were asked to list what they thought were the present Seven Wonders of the World. Though there were some disagreements, the following received the most votes:

1. Egypt's Great Pyramids
2. Taj Mahal
3. Grand Canyon
4. Panama Canal
5. Empire State Building
6. St. Peter's Basilica
7. China's Great Wall

While gathering the votes, the teacher noted that one quiet student hadn't turned in her paper yet. So she asked the girl if she was having trouble with her list.

The girl replied, "Yes, a little. I couldn't quite make up my mind because there were so many."

The teacher said, "Well, tell us what you have, and maybe we can help."

The girl hesitated, then read, "I think the Seven Wonders of the World are:

1. To see
2. To hear
3. To touch
4. To taste
5. To feel
6. To laugh
7. To love."

The room was so quiet you could have heard a pin drop. The things we overlook as simple, ordinary and taken for granted are truly wondrous! A gentle reminder – the most precious things in life cannot be built by hand or bought by man.

I recently was speaking at an American Cancer Society Survivor Dinner. As part of my keynote speech, I asked the audience, most of whom were survivors, to list out the Seven Wonders of the World. Over eighty percent of them listed life. What about you? Are you missing the best parts of the trip by looking for some magical destination that will outdistance you? Are you looking for happiness in *something* or *someone*? When I was around twelve and on vacation with my mother, she asked me a question I will always remember. She asked me if the sunset that we were watching made me happy. When I didn't respond, she simply said, "In this lifetime if the sun setting doesn't bring you joy and it takes a house, a car, or someone else, then chances are you will always struggle to be happy." Her point was well stated. If you want to change the way you live and experience the true joy of life, then check your passion, cure your destination disease, follow the directions, remember the rainbow, dare to be different, and refocus your attention. If you do, I can promise you will *enjoy the ride!*

THE ABC'S FOR YOUR TRIP

Always do more than you are expected to do.

Believe in yourself.

Cure your destination disease.

Don't fear what you want the most.

Expect the best.

Focus on things you can control and affect.

Give life's precious moments value; share them.

Hang on when others let go.

Imagine yourself succeeding.

Jump over problems; don't go around them.

Keep saying no to the good, so you can say yes to the best.

Look for opportunities, not guarantees.

Make yesterday the deadline for all complaints.

Never give someone permission to ruin your day.

Omit the word can't from your vocabulary.

Pursue your passion.

Quit worrying about change; anticipate it and accept it.

Refocus your attention.

Strive for perfection.

Take quiet time.

Unfurl your wings and start flying.

Visualize it to realize it.

When your ship comes in, be willing to unload it.

Xpect some things to go wrong; just don't go with them.

Yearn to be the best in everything you do.

Zero in on today: tomorrow will outdistance you.